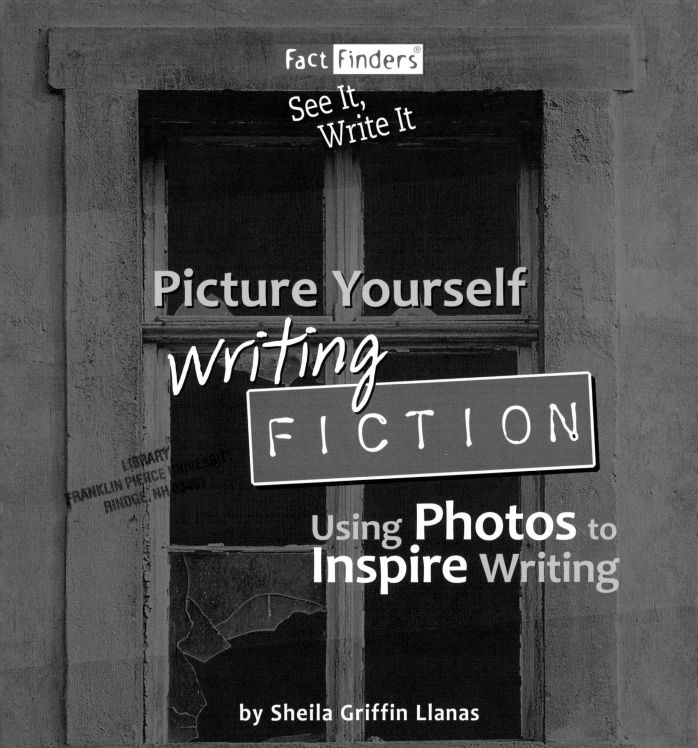

Fact Finders®

See It,
Write It

Picture Yourself
writing
FICTION

Using **Photos** to **Inspire** Writing

by Sheila Griffin Llanas

CAPSTONE PRESS
a capstone imprint

Fact Finders are published by Capstone Press,
151 Good Counsel Drive, P.O. Box 669, Mankato, Minnesota 56002.
www.capstonepub.com

Library of Congress Cataloging-in-Publication Data
Llanas, Sheila Griffin, 1958–
  Picture yourself writing fiction : using photos to inspire writing / by Sheila Griffin Llanas.
  p. cm.—(Fact finders. see it, write it)
  Includes bibliographical references and index.
  Summary: "Useful tips and writing prompts show young writers how to use images to inspire fiction
writing"—Provided by publisher.
  ISBN 978-1-4296-6127-0 (library binding)
  ISBN 978-1-4296-7205-4 (paperback)
  1. Fiction—Authorship—Juvenile literature. 2. Literature and photography—Juvenile literature. I. Title.
  PN3355.L55 2012
  808.3—dc22   2010052357

Editorial Credits

Jennifer Besel, editor; Veronica Correia, designer; Eric Manske, production specialist

Photo Credits

Dreamstime: Shariff Che'Lah, 7, Vladimir Ovchinnikov, 1, 22; iStockphoto: graham heywood, 21,
kutay tanir, 15, Vetta/David Kerkhoff, cover, 24-25, Vetta/Enrico Flanchini, 8; Shutterstock: Darius
Pabrinkis, 27, Devid Camerlynck, 17, Eric Gevaert, 26, J van der Wolf, 23, Jeanne Hatch, 19, JGW
Images, 28, Joggie Botma, 12, Kailash K Soni, 6, Khoroshunova Olga, 5, Kletr, 3, 13, littlesam, 16,
Morozova Oxana, 9, Regien Paassen, 11, St. Nick, 18, Studio 1One, 20, VOJTa Herout, 14, zooropa,
10; Victoria Reichow, 32

Printed in the United States of America in Stevens Point, Wisconsin.
032011   006111WZF11

TABLE OF CONTENTS

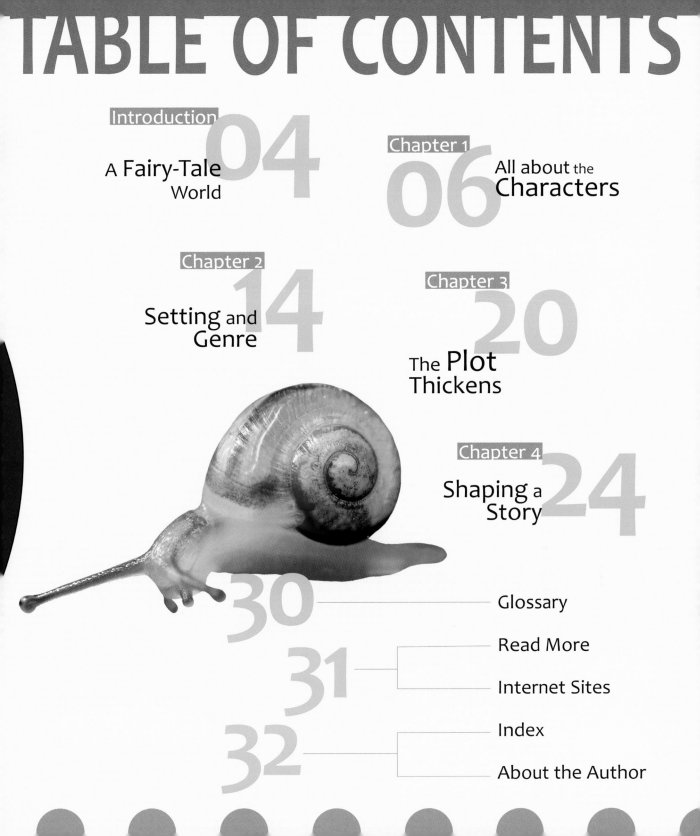

A *Fairy-Tale* World

Have you ever read a book that you just couldn't put down?

Great books start with great ideas. Fiction authors create **vivid** images with words. But crafting vivid scenes and lively dialogue can be difficult sometimes. That's where pictures can help. Some photos look like scenes right out of a story. When you look at a photo, you might wonder, "How did that happen? What will happen next?"

The answers you create for those questions could be the key to unlocking a stunning story.

The evil sorceress had turned Princess Sana into a goldfish. Sana hid behind reeds in the freezing water. She waved her new fins. She had to swim back to the castle.

vivid—sharp and clear

The Writing Process

Step 1 Prewrite

Plan what you're going to write. Are you going to write a fictional story, a poem, or some other form of writing? Choose a topic, and start brainstorming details. Also identify your audience and the purpose of your piece.

Step 2 Draft

Put your ideas on paper. Start crafting your composition. Don't worry about getting the punctuation and grammar perfect. Just start writing.

Step 4 Edit

Now look for those pesky punctuation errors. Also check your spelling, grammar, and capitalization.

Step 3 Revise

Check your work for ways to improve your writing. Fix areas that are confusing. Look for spots that need reorganizing. Are there places where you could make the words more clear or exciting? Having other people look at your work might be helpful too.

Step 5 Publish

When you're done, share your work! You can present it to a class or post it online. Maybe you could have it printed in your school newspaper. The possibilities for sharing your work are endless.

Chapter 1

ALL ABOUT THE CHARACTERS

Main Character

Every story needs a main character (MC). The MC is the key player in whatever happens in your tale. Photos can help jump-start an idea for an MC.

Look at the girl in this picture. Who is she? What's behind her secretive smile? As an author, you get to answer those questions however you'd like.

As ideas come to you, write them in a profile chart. Create details about the MC's **backstory**. Also include information about her family or home life. To make a believable character, make sure your details and backstory make sense together.

Profile Chart

Topic	Details
Name	Chaaya (means Shadow)
Age	15, but acts older than her age
Home	Mumbai, India, but now her family lives in Pennsylvania
Backstory	After they moved, Chaaya's older sister, Amrita, ran away. Her father is furious.
Secret	Chaaya got a letter from Amrita.
Goal	to find Amrita

When your profile is complete, use it to craft a story. Make your MC real by sprinkling in details from the profile. Use the backstory to explain why your MC acts a certain way.

backstory—a story that tells what happened before the main story

write about It!

Bring the man in this photo to life. Create his profile. Add rows for topics such as his favorite food, favorite color, hobbies, job, pets, and friends. Stretch your imagination. Add as many details as you can think of. You never know which ones you will use.

Secondary characters

A story would be pretty boring if the MC had no one to talk to.

Your MC needs a best friend, a worst enemy, or even a pet. Any character that **interacts** with the MC is a secondary character (SC).

A good way to develop an SC is to start with his or her backstory. How did the secondary character meet the MC? Is their relationship good or bad?

Create a backstory chart to explore different ideas for the same characters. Photos can help inspire you here too. Imagine that your MC is the person on the left of this picture. Who's the person next to him? Create a chart to explore the possibilities.

Secondary Character	Backstory
Colin, a loyal-to-the-end friend	grew up as MC's best friend; promised to play in MC's band
Eric, an angry rival	wanted to play lead guitar but got stuck playing backup; insists on being the lead

Once the chart is done, you have an important decision to make. Which idea inspires you most? That's the SC to use. Then create a profile chart for the secondary character.

The more details you have for all your characters, the easier it will be to write about them.

write about It!

Your MC is on a trip thousands of miles from home. The MC looks down from the top of a spiral stone staircase. Suddenly, _____ appears.

Who appears? Friend or foe? And where? Perhaps the secondary character is at the bottom of the staircase. Maybe he or she is behind the MC's shoulder. Explore ideas for an SC by filling in a backstory chart.

Then choose your favorite idea. Write a few sentences of a story about the characters' meeting. Is your MC happy to see the secondary character? Use details from the backstory chart to explain the characters' reactions.

interact—to have action between people, groups, or things

Dialogue

Dialogue lets characters share information in their own words. It's a powerful tool.

Readers can learn a lot about a character by what he or she says. You can make characters express courage, blurt confessions, or show their evil sides.

Photos can help you imagine dialogue. Stare at a photo until you hear the words the subjects might say.

"Whoa! So that's what Ty is hiding."

"I should have worn armpit pads."

"Get down! If they know we saw they'll ... I don't know what they'll do."

The best fiction stories use surprising dialogue to make readers gasp. In your writing, try to think of unexpected twists that could happen in a conversation.

"You broke Mr. Denver's window," Jake said. "He's going to be so mad at you."

"Not when he finds your baseball in his living room," A. J. said.

"What are you talking about?" asked Jake.

"That ball had your name on it!"

write about It!

In fiction anything can talk, even rocks, trees, and animals. Practice writing dialogue by letting these camels do the talking. Try to share funny or surprising information through their conversation. Need inspiration? Find a friend, and pretend you are the camels. Have a conversation. Write down your best lines of dialogue.

Once you have some dialogue, build a story around it. Describe what events led up to the conversation and what happens next.

Point of View

In your writing, you'll need to decide who or what will tell the story. Will the MC talk to readers? Or will you have a narrator?

The way you tell the story is the **point of view** (POV). The POV shapes what readers learn. Readers will only know what the character telling the story sees, hears, and feels.

A photo can inspire POV options. A picture is taken from one POV. But you can imagine other views. Take this picture of skydivers, for example.

You could tell a story from the POV of the pilot, a skydiver, or a person on the ground below. All three people would see events differently.

Once you choose which character's story you'll tell, you have another choice to make. You could write the story as if you're telling what happened to someone else. This is called third-person POV.

DAN WAS LYiNG UNDER A TREE, WATCHiNG SKYDiVERS FLOAT TO EARTH.

Another option is to write the story as if it happened to you. This is first-person POV. In first person, you use words like "I" and "me."

I WAS LYiNG UNDER A TREE, WATCHiNG THE SKYDiVERS FLOAT TO EARTH.

point of view—the way someone or something looks at or thinks about something

Write about It!

A sticky snail tips toward the water. What does the snail see and feel? What does it think, hear, taste, and smell? Write a paragraph describing the snail's POV.

Then switch it up. Write paragraphs from other points of view. Here are some ideas to get you started.

1. A HIDDEN FISH—How would a fish spying on the snail feel?

2. ANOTHER CREATURE—How would a much bigger or smaller creature see the snail?

3. THE REFLECTION—What if the snail's watery image could talk?

Do you feel an idea for a good story brewing?
START WRITING!

Chapter 2

SETTING AND GENRE

setting

A dungeon is an intense setting for action, **suspense**, or romance. The setting is where a story happens. Where you put your characters plays a big part in the story. A scary story wouldn't seem as frightening in a brightly lit room. To create setting, pretend you're in a photo. Describe the setting with words that appeal to the senses.

Sensory details will make readers feel like they are in that scary place.

SIGHT: Shadows blanketed the long hallway.

SOUND: The hinges popped as the door closed.

SMELL: The air reeked of smoke.

TOUCH: A light breeze prickled like spiders on her skin.

TASTE: The dense smoke tasted like coal.

THE DUNGEON DOORS CREAKED OPEN ONTO A DIM HALLWAY.

suspense—an anxious and uncertain feeling
sensory—having to do with the five senses

write about It!

Let this photo inspire a setting. How does it feel to ride on a fast-moving train? What smells fill the train? What scenery rushes past? What do the tracks sound like? Write a paragraph or two, describing the train ride in words that appeal to all five senses.

Genre

There are many categories of fiction writing. You've heard of adventure, romance, western, and fantasy books. These categories are called genres (ZHAN-ruhz).

Choosing your story's genre before you start writing is a good idea. The genre helps you focus your writing style. Scary descriptions work for horror but not for fairy tales. Fast-paced action makes for great suspense. Trees can talk in fantasy, but they can't in **realism**.

Sometimes story ideas come from the genres a photo inspires. When you look at a photo, make a list of every kind of story you can think of. One photo could inspire ideas in three or more genres.

MYSTERY—Finding a purse on the tracks, Glenda runs to the train station to tell the police. Instead, she finds the thief. "I'll take that," he says.

PARANORMAL—Glenda waves, but the 9:05 train passengers don't wave back. "A ghost train," Glenda whispers as a bone-chilling breeze rushes past.

ROMANCE—Glenda skips to the station. She can't wait to greet Nick when he steps off the train. After six long months, he is finally coming home.

write about It!

Gaze at the castle. Do you see a story coming from deep within its walls? Make a list of the different genres and story ideas that come to mind. When you have a list, decide which story you'd most like to read. Then write it. As you write the story, keep your genre in mind.

Make sure the setting, time period, and dialogue fit the genre you chose.

For a challenge, rewrite your story to fit a new genre. Change a fairy tale into science fiction. Transform a mystery into a comedy. You might be surprised by your creativity.

realism—a genre of writing that does not use fantasy of any kind
paranormal—a genre of writing that deals with topics that can't be explained by science

Time Periods

Some stories take place long ago. Some take place far in the future. The time period you choose affects how characters look, act, and talk. It also affects what setting you choose.

Photos can transport you to time periods of the past. If photos like this inspire you, consider writing historical fiction. In historical fiction, you use real-life details. To write historical fiction, you'll have to do some research.

Look for **sources** that have information about how people dressed, spoke, and lived during your time period. Real details make historical fiction believable. Knights, for example, traveled by horseback. Cars did not exist in the Middle Ages.

Sir Garin spurred his horse toward the castle. His armor clanked. "Thieves approach," muttered the knight. "I must tell the Queen."

source—someone or something that provides information

18

write about It!

Cowboys roping. Horses galloping. Are you feeling inspired? Let this photo bring you back to the Old West. Do some research to find out what cowboys in the Old West wore and ate. Discover where they slept. What kind of work did they do?

Use your research to write a fictional story about cowboy life. Create a cowboy character, describe the setting, and bring the time period to life. Help readers feel like they have been transported to the Wild West.

Chapter 3

THE PLOT THICKENS

Plot

A man's muscles strain. His sweaty hands grip the rope. But photos can't tell a complete story. How did the man end up here? Will he reach the top, or will he fall?

Making up answers to those questions is a great way to develop plot. Plot is the events that happen in a story. Try writing a plot summary to organize the order in which events happen.

1. Luke's brother dared him to climb Pike's Rock.
2. Luke tried to climb the sheer rock by himself.
3. He slipped and almost fell.
4. Terrified, he dragged himself onto a ledge.
5. When he reached the top, he found his brother, smiling, holding the rope.

Photos capture great action moments.

Once you have a summary, it's easier to build the whole story. You simply expand each main point. Explain who was involved. Decide when and where things happened. Use dialogue to share information. And don't forget sensory details to make readers feel like they're part of the action.

write about It!

Let this action inspire a story. What led up to this race? Who wins and who loses? Write a plot summary to outline the action. Then go back and develop your characters, setting, and time period. When you have all the pieces, expand them into a full story.

Problems

A **good** plot often starts with a **bad** problem.

It might sound odd, but conflicts improve plots. Everybody has problems. Maybe that's why we like reading about great characters with big troubles. Try starting a story with a conflict. Include who's involved, when it's happening, and where the action takes place.

Photos can show problems. But they don't always explain what caused them. A broken window is a problem, but how did it happen? You get to answer that question. Don't settle for everyday explanations. Push yourself to come up with a twist that will grab readers' attention.

On the day of the field trip, Malia found herself
(when)   (MC)   (POV)

bolting through the museum with a guard chasing her.
(where)   (SC)

"Stop that kid!" the guard yelled. "She broke a window!"
(dialogue)   (conflict)

write about It!

This photo captures a problem in midaction. The fire is already raging out of control. Make a list of at least 10 ways the fire might have started. These ideas could be the start of 10 very different stories! Choose your favorite idea, and write a story about this conflict. Make sure your story explains who, what, when, where, why, and how.

Chapter 4

SHAPING A STORY

Story Arc

A story is like a puzzle. The plot, characters, and conflicts are pieces. But how do you fit the pieces into one story? Authors follow a diagram called a story arc. A story arc shows how a story should flow from beginning to end. Most stories follow this simple plan.

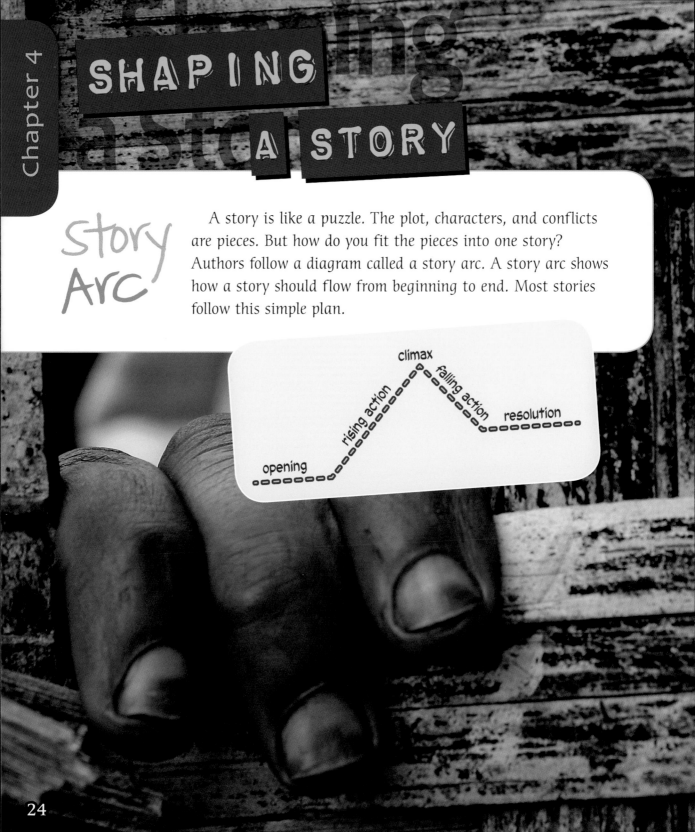

opening · rising action · climax · falling action · resolution

The steps in a story arc help you keep the plot moving. A photo can inspire any step in a story arc. Look at this photo of a boy. Who is he? Where is he? What put that look in his eye? Use your answers to create ideas for the steps in a story arc.

1. OPENiNG—INTRODUCE YOUR MC.

Bring in your MC and a secondary character or two. Describe setting and time period.

"Let's go fishing," Becker typed from the dock.

"OK," Uncle Myles texted back. "Meet me on deck in five minutes."

Becker sat aboard the old boat, waiting.

2. RiSiNG ACTiON—CREATE A CONFLiCT.

Maybe the MC makes a mistake. Or make up a problem the MC can't control. Whatever the problem, it should get readers on the edge of their seats.

Two strange men jumped aboard. Becker ducked into a fish crate, trapped, as the men drove the boat to sea. Becker sputtered in the icy spray. "A stowaway!" one man growled, spotting Becker in the crate.

To connect parts of a story, try setting two or more photos side by side. Think up ways to get your character from one picture to the next. Surprising plots are sure to develop!

3. CLIMAX —YOUR STORY REACHES THE MOST EXCITING POINT.

The characters are at the height of the action. This part should have readers' hearts pounding.

Becker burst from the crate and lurched to the cabin. "Mayday!" he shouted into the radio. One man lunged for Becker. Becker kicked him. "Leave him," the other man called. "Let's go!"

4. FALLING ACTION—AFTER THE CLIMAX, THE ACTION STARTS TO COOL DOWN.

In this step, the MC deals with what just happened. He or she surveys the damage and picks up the pieces.

The boat thieves leapt overboard and sped off in a waiting motorboat. Becker slowed the boat and his beating heart. Over the pounding waves, the radio crackled, "Help is on the way."

5. RESOLUTION—THIS IS THE END.

Usually, a story closes in a meaningful way. Whether the ending is happy or sad, the MC is changed. His or her life will never be the same.

"Those criminals made that a getaway boat, son," said the Coast Guard officer, handing a blanket to Becker. "You're lucky to be alive." Becker shuddered. He knew the officer was right.

write about It!

Here is a broken bicycle. Does this image make you think of falling action and picking up the pieces? Maybe this picture sparks an idea for a conflict to get the action rising. Using this photo for inspiration, create plot ideas for each of the five steps in a story arc. When you're done, use your story arc to craft a stunning tale full of details, dialogue, and action.

A Spark Becomes a Flame

Stories can come from anywhere.

Images are one great tool to get your mind going. Image is the first word in imagination, after all!

You can find story-starting photos all over. Magazines, billboards, and catalogs are just a few spots to look. You could even page back through this book. Let new story ideas spring from the photos. And don't be afraid to mix it up. Overlap people from one photo onto the setting of another. Let the people and animals from separate photos meet.

Every photo has the potential to spark the next great novel. What stories do you see beyond the photos' borders? Let a tiny story idea grow as you write the words down. Just take it one step at a time, and let the story begin.

write about It!

What do you imagine as you look at this picture? Is it a beginning or an end? Maybe it suggests rising action, or falling. Let your imagination run wild. Develop characters and backstory. Choose a point of view, setting, and time period. Sprinkle in dialogue and description. Stir in action. Turn each step in the story arc into a section of the story. When you fit all the pieces together, you'll have a work of art.

GLOSSARY

backstory (BAK-stor-ee)—a story that tells what happened before the main story

interact (in-tur-AKT)—to have action between people, groups, or things

narrator (na-RATE-or)—a character who tells a story or describes an event

paranormal (pair-uh-NOR-muhl)—a genre of writing that deals with topics that can't be explained by science

point of view (POINT UV VYOO)—the way someone or something looks at or thinks about something

realism (REE-uh-liz-uhm)—a genre of writing that does not use fantasy of any kind

sensory (SEN-suh-ree)—having to do with the five senses

source (SORSS)—someone or something that provides information

suspense (suh-SPENSS)—an anxious or uncertain feeling caused by having to wait to see what happens

vivid (VIV-id)—sharp and clear

READ MORE

McGuinness, Denis E. and Lauren Spencer. *Writing to Describe.* Write Like a Pro. New York: Rosen Central, 2012.

McKay, Laura Lee. *Write Fantasy Fiction in 5 Simple Steps.* Creative Writing in 5 Simple Steps. Berkeley Heights, N.J.: Enslow Publishers, 2012.

Warren, Celia. *How to Write Stories.* How to Write. Laguna Hills, Calif.: QEB Pub., 2007.

INTERNET SITES

FactHound offers a safe, fun way to find Internet sites related to this book. All of the sites on FactHound have been researched by our staff.

Here's all you do:

Visit *www.facthound.com*

Type in this code: 9781429661270

Super-cool stuff!

Check out projects, games and lots more at
www.capstonekids.com

INDEX

ABOUT THE AUTHOR

Sheila Griffin Llanas is a poet, essayist, fiction author, and educational writer. She teaches writing at the University of Wisconsin-Waukesha. For seven summers, she taught writing for the Center for Talented Youth with the Johns Hopkins University. She writes nonfiction books for children and teens for Capstone Press and other publishers. She has a Bachelor of Arts degree in literature and a Master of Fine Arts degree in poetry.

DATE DUE

GAYLORD   PRINTED IN U.S.A.